GREENPEACE

MARION KOZAK

(SERIES EDITOR: ROB ALCRAFT)

Heinemann
LIBRARY

First published in Great Britain by Heinemann Library
Halley Court, Jordan Hill, Oxford OX2 8EJ
a division of Reed Educational and Professional Publishing Ltd

OXFORD FLORENCE PRAGUE MADRID ATHENS
MELBOURNE AUCKLAND KUALA LUMPUR SINGAPORE TOKYO
IBADAN NAIROBI KAMPALA JOHANNESBURG GABORONE
PORTSMOUTH NH CHICAGO MEXICO CITY SAO PAULO

A 3% royalty on all copies of this book sold by Heinemann Library will be donated to Greenpeace Environmental Trust, a registered charity, number 284934.

Produced by Plum Creative (01590 612970)
Printed in China

01 00 99 98 97
10 9 8 7 6 5 4 3 2 1

ISBN 0 431 02749 8

British Library Cataloguing in Publication Data
    Kozak, Marion
    Greenpeace. - (Taking Action)
    1. Greenpeace - Juvenile literature
    I.Title
    363.7' 0526

The views expressed in this book are those of Greenpeace and do not necessarily represent the views of Heinemann Library, Reed Educational and Professional Publishing, nor the series editor.

Acknowledgements
The publishers would like to thank the following for permission to reproduce photographs:
Randi Baird p28; Antonello Bello p29; Bill Barclay p4; Daniel Beltra p24; Kayte Brimacombe pp11,14,15; Robert Brook p5; Kristien Buyse pp5,20; Steve Cox p26; Michael Dean p22; Bernd Euler p13; D Grace p7; Jim Hodges p10; Jim Hodson pp9,17,29; David Hoffman pp19, 21; Steve Morgan pp23,25; Robert Morris pp10,18; Gavin Newman p13; Peter Northolt pp13,17; Oldham Evening Chronicle p8; C Plowden p7; David Sims pp12,13,27; Dieter Vennemann p8.

Cover photograph by Dorreboone.
Cover illustration by Scott Rhodes.

Every effort has been made to contact copyright holders of any material reproduced in this book. Any omissions will be rectified in subsequent printings if notice is given to the publisher.

All words in the text appearing in bold like **this** are explained in the Glossary.

CONTENTS

WHAT'S THE PROBLEM?

The planet Earth and its creatures are under threat. We use the Earth's resources too carelessly. Cars and lorries pump out poisonous gases, and the oil, gas and coal we burn to produce electricity pollutes the atmosphere. Now scientists from all over the world are worried that this **pollution** will cause **global warming**. It may mean the world's weather will change, and there will be more floods, storms and hurricanes.

▼ *Clearcutting* **of Clayoquot Sound in British Columbia, Canada, has destroyed some of the largest and oldest trees. The cutting of these** *temperate rainforests* **destroys rare plants, disturbs the rivers where salmon breed and threatens eagles and bears.**

DANGER TO THE PLANET

At the same time we dump poisonous chemicals and waste from our factories and farms onto land and into rivers, lakes and seas. This pollution passes from waste tips into rivers and seas, into food eaten by animals and humans. We also overuse our natural resources by chopping down forests which for years have provided a home for animals and plants. Many of the **environments** we are damaging or destroying are unique, and once they are gone we will not be able to replace them.

Greenpeace wants to persuade industry, agriculture and energy producers to change to **clean production**, and think about the future of the planet Earth. This means producing goods and food which cause as little damage to the environment as possible.

One acre of forest is destroyed every 12 seconds.

Perhaps the worst thing about *toxic* pollution is that it can contaminate *plankton* in the sea, which serves as food for fish.

◄ Greenpeace protesters holding oiled birds at the European Union Environment and Transport meeting. All oil tankers leak oil but accidents make matters much worse: the *Sea Empress* spilled 70,000 tonnes of crude oil off Milford Haven in 1996 risking the lives of fish, birds and other marine life.

The Western Antarctic ice sheet is melting due to increased temperatures.

WHAT DOES GREENPEACE DO?

Greenpeace was set up 25 years ago, by people who were horrified by the prospect of nuclear war and wanted to stop the testing of **nuclear weapons**. They called the new organization 'Greenpeace' because of their vision of a **green** planet and peace on Earth. They soon realized that as well as nuclear testing there were other threats to life on Earth. Their next action was to defend whales and seals, which were being killed for commercial markets. Since then, Greenpeace has expanded its activities to try to protect animals, plants, humans and planet Earth from destruction.

'You can't sink a rainbow' is a Greenpeace motto. The *Rainbow Warrior* is the Greenpeace flagship, which has been involved in many important campaigns. The rainbow symbolizes the beauty of the Earth and the dove is an emblem of peace.

Greenpeace organize peaceful **protests** to show that taking risks with life on Earth is wrong. They want to protect large species such as whales and dolphins, as well as tiny creatures like sand-eels, which are basic food for birds and bigger fish.

▶ British protesters adding their voice to Greenpeace anti-nuclear campaigns. The Nevada Desert was a nuclear test site for the USA and UK before a ban was agreed in 1996.

6

Almost 2000 nuclear tests took place before the ban in 1996.

Greenpeace protesters dressed up as puffins to protest at the Houses of Parliament about the lack of controls on industrial sand-eel fishing. Greenpeace persuaded several big food companies to use vegetable oil, instead of fish oil from sand-eels, in biscuits and margarine.

Harpooning whales was common practice in the 1970s, when Greenpeace took up its campaign to stop whaling. Commercial whaling is now banned, but Norway and Japan still hunt whales, and campaigns to stop them doing this are still being held.

7

In 1995, the world-wide protest eventually stopped French nuclear testing in the Pacific.

HOW GREENPEACE WORKS

Greenpeace has offices in 32 countries and an international co-ordinating team in Amsterdam, in The Netherlands. Older Greenpeace organizations help the newly established ones, and they support each other in important campaigns and emergencies. For example, in 1986 the Chernobyl nuclear power station in Ukraine exploded. Greenpeace organizations around the world helped set up Greenpeace in Ukraine, which campaigns for alternatives to **nuclear energy**.

Children take part in sponsored swims for Greenpeace. Many others write in to the office to say: 'I want to save the world from being destroyed.'

MONEY FROM SUPPORTERS

In the UK, Greenpeace raises about £8 million per year in subscriptions and donations from the public. This helps to pay for a fleet of boats, the UK national office and international activities. Greenpeace does not take any money from governments or businesses. This gives it freedom to protest against destructive practices by anyone, anywhere.

The Greenpeace action bus on tour in St Petersburg, Russia. Equipped as a mobile laboratory, it toured Russia and the Baltic States measuring sea and river *pollution*.

The Greenpeace UK office has paid staff and volunteers who organize **protest** actions. They are also in charge of scientific investigations, public information and press work. Finding solutions to **environmental problems** is very important to Greenpeace. It does this by looking for alternatives to polluting substances like **PVC** or **fossil fuels**.

Greenpeace activities are supported solely by donations.

A sign flashed by Greenpeace onto Big Ben in London reminds people about the dangers of all nuclear energy. The Chernobyl accident happened far away in Ukraine, and 400,000 people had to be moved away from the area. Even in the UK there are still controls on the sale and slaughter of 317,000 sheep affected by radioactive material which has been carried from Chernobyl over 2400 km in the air.

26th APRIL 1986

REMEMBER CHERNOBYL

Chernobyl caused a seven-fold increase in thyroid cancer in Ukraine.

MEET PETER MELCHETT
GREENPEACE DIRECTOR

I have been director of Greenpeace since 1989. Every day is different. My job is to make sure that all our activities fit together like a jigsaw.

I like coming into our office, which is light and airy. We have hung white sheets on the ceilings to keep the noise down. Our windows look out on a wildlife garden.

For a lot of my adult life I have worked in environmental organizations. Working for Greenpeace is different because we are truly international. The fact that the name is familiar to a lot of people means that we can ask for support and expect to be heard. We are always in contact with the 32 Greenpeace offices on our computer network, called Greenlink.

7.00am Off by train to Aberdeen where our local group has organized a **protest** against whaling by Norway.

10.30am I join the local group for the protest. All kinds of whales have been hunted to near-extinction and now the smallest minke whale is being killed for profit despite the prohibition of whaling by the International Whaling Commission.

▲ **I learn so much from our local group in Aberdeen. Whale meat is sold for £290 per kilo in some countries like Japan. No wonder Norway wants to double the number it kills.**

Only about 1000 blue whales have survived out of 220,000.

 At the Greenpeace Business Conference companies discussed ways to phase out harmful chemicals like *PVC*.

Greenpeace has been campaigning against commercial whaling ever since the organization's early days. After 25 years the number of whales being killed has dropped from tens of thousands a year to around 1000. It is a tragedy that Japan and Norway are still killing whales.

4.30pm Back at the office, I change into a suit to meet company directors at an important meeting to discuss our programme of **green** solutions to industrial pollution, like **greenfreeze**.

5.00pm My colleague Chris Rose and I suggest how we could work with the companies to find solutions to the problems facing us. Some companies are beginning to accept our point of view and help us. It has been a typical Greenpeace day, protesting with groups in the morning and talking with businesses in the afternoon.

Travelling by bike is a great way to save energy and keep fit!

MEET AL BAKER
CAMPAIGNER

This summer we are patrolling the Wee Bankie, 32 km off the east coast of Scotland, to stop the fishing for sand-eels.

The Wee Bankie is alive with thousands of puffins, guillemots, dolphins, minke whales, shoals of porpoise and herds of seals, all depending in some way on the tiny sand-eels. I love being in boats, mostly in inflatable dinghies. That was my job during the Brent Spar campaign and in the protest against French nuclear tests in the South Pacific. But climbing is my real joy. Mostly I climb mountains but also a fair number of buildings on Greenpeace missions!

▲ **We patrol the Wee Bankie in our dinghy before the Danish industrial fishing fleet arrives. Yesterday the Danish crew tried to spear our dinghy with hooks and knives attached to poles. It was scary.**

5.30am The volunteers get into their protective orange survival suits and wait on board for instructions. As the fishing vessel comes into view we are lowered into our inflatable dinghies by crane. It's a slow and dangerous operation.

700,000 tonnes of sand-eels are hoovered up by fishing boats every year.

6.00am Three of us jump into the water with our buoys and sausage-shaped boom, designed to get in the way of the fishing boats. We also carry signs which say 'Stop North Sea over-fishing'.

6.30am Suddenly more Danish fishing boats and a British one appear. Soon there are five, playing a cat-and-mouse game with us. They chase the inflatable dinghies and shoot flares at us. Luckily, inflatables can get around more easily than big boats and we manage to nip in and out of the line of fire. The Danish vessels are busy trying to ram our boat, the *MV Sirius*.

4.00pm Back on board the *MV Sirius*. A message comes from the captain of one of the Danish ships: 'If you don't give up now we will sink you.' Our skipper cannot take the risk and as the Danish ship gives chase, we head off to safer waters in UK territory.

▲ **Industrial 'hoover' fishing uses very fine nets which scoop up huge amounts of sand-eels. These tiny fish are valuable food for fish such as cod, haddock and whiting, sea birds and other marine wildlife. If sand-eels are destroyed, so are the other fish.**

6.00pm Good news. Wildlife groups, MPs, ocean experts and Scottish fishermen's organizations have sent messages of support for our campaign. We will be back every day while the industrial fishing season lasts.

◀ **Our group swimming out with buoys to try to stop the boats from fishing. All we have is our long inflatable boom, to try to stop the fishing vessels.**

Industrial fishing threatens all marine creatures that feed on sand-eels.

MEET BRENDA RAMSEY
SOLAR CAMPAIGNER

Campaigning is second nature to me. My job at Greenpeace is to spread the word that the sun can provide us with more than half of the electricity that we need. I go round the country talking to people, including children, politicians, technicians and people from industry.

I am delighted with our new **solar-powered** kitchen, which shows that it is possible to cook, wash clothes, refrigerate food, and in short do anything that needs electricity, using the sun's energy.

We are going to travel round the country to get public support for our solar energy campaign. Today is our first public appearance, in London's Greenwich Park.

▶ **Setting up the solar panels on our kitchen van was amazingly simple. If everyone had them there would be much less need for *fossil fuel* and nuclear power stations.**

6.00am First stop is our warehouse, where the kitchen is kept under wraps. I can't wait to get it out into the open where it will stand proudly next to the 19th-century sailing ship, the *Cutty Sark*.

8.00am It is a beautiful sunny day and lots of people are about. People are curious about the panels, which provide electricity for the machines in the same way as a normal electricity supply. Everyone can see how the panels trap sunlight, even on cloudy days.

14

Solar panels could provide two-thirds of electricity needs.

11.00am We offer breakfast with freshly squeezed orange juice and toast. We welcome people aboard. Soon they are looking around, and some children ask me to wash their T-shirts, which I gladly do.

2.00pm 'We want a solar kitchen, too' says a little boy. I tell him that rooftop solar panels could be fitted to his home. The more panels you have, the more electricity you will get.

5.00pm There are loads of children on board and I show them how to make popcorn using electricity from the sun. 'Tastes just as good as ordinary popcorn,' they say. Time to pack up our van for the night. Next stop, Liverpool.

▲ **Our kitchen van is painted orange and yellow like the sun's rays, which are freely available but not fully used. Squeezing fresh oranges on our solar squeezer convinces our visitors that going solar works.**

▼ **Having convinced the children, the next step is to persuade builders, engineers and politicians that this is a good idea.**

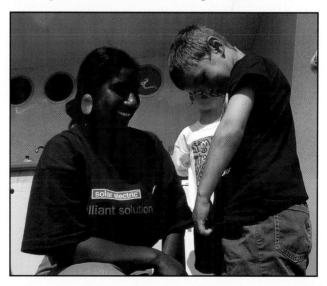

24 solar panels are enough for an average house.

MEET MIRELLA VON LINDENFELS PRESS OFFICER

My job as press officer is to give information and help TV, radio and newspapers write and broadcast about Greenpeace activities. One minute a journalist wants information about a leak from a nuclear power station, the next minute someone wants to know about the North Sea fish crisis.

Today Greenpeace is protesting in front of the Unilever building against **genetic manipulation** of soya beans. The result of this manipulation will be a soya bean that can resist weedkiller, but nobody knows what it might do to plant or human life. So Greenpeace is calling for a ban, especially as soya beans are used in nearly two-thirds of processed foods like bread and margarine.

7.00am We arrive at the Greenpeace office and I explain to the volunteers about being photographed. Then the make-up people whiten their faces and paint black Xs on them to represent genetic manipulation. Other Greenpeace offices in Europe will be organizing similar protests.

▲ **These volunteers from local groups are protesting against the use of genetically manipulated soya beans in the production of our food.**

8.00am I set off to meet the journalists. We don't want Unilever to know about our **protest** action yet. I wait round the corner for a call to tell me when everybody is in place.

8.30am The group looks fantastic. The white-faced X people are suitably grim, and loud sci-fi music from the TV programme *The X Files* is blaring in the local underground station.

Every day, British farmers spread juggernaut-loads of chemicals on the land.

The TV cameras have arrived and lots of people are milling around as they go to work. Two Greenpeace protesters have climbed the Unilever building and hung their banner saying 'Don't genetically experiment with us'.

6.00pm It was a good day, sending a clear message which I hope will be mentioned in some of the national daily papers. Tomorrow I have to contact all the magazines and weeklies.

The message is loud and clear: consumers want to know which food is genetically manipulated.

9.00am My job is to make sure that the newspaper, TV and radio people who come to the event get all the information about why Greenpeace is protesting. People are genuinely interested. They don't want to buy genetically manipulated food.

10.00am The TV crews and photographers have got everything they need now and I have to rush back to the office, where I spend the day on other stories and questions from journalists that need my attention.

Almost two-thirds of Europeans don't want to eat genetically engineered food.

WORK WITH LOCAL GROUPS

The most important people in Greenpeace activities are its 280,000 supporters. Some of them take part in national campaigns. They all care about the **environment** and give their spare time to campaigns and protests.

Once a year several hundred group members get together for a weekend conference, to discuss Greenpeace issues, plan future actions and share ideas. They receive training on how to work more effectively together. 'It's seeing so many other people out there pushing for change that spurs you on. I feel more valuable to Greenpeace now than before,' said one member at the conference.

▼ Sometimes bands perform without a fee and give the profits from sold tickets to charity. Here Pink Floyd are thanked for raising £1 million for Greenpeace and other organizations.

There are 150 local Greenpeace groups throughout the UK.

RAISING THE MONEY

Some members help in demonstrations, and collect money for Greenpeace. They hold sponsored walks, swims, cycle rides, canoeing and even running marathons. Money also comes from collection tins in shops, schools and public places. Sometimes, a pop group will organize a concert and donate the profits to Greenpeace. Many families join Greenpeace, and the children get involved in group activities like running information stalls and selling shirts, diaries, Christmas cards and posters.

▲ **Ben Elton and his young friends Trev and Simon opening the sponsored 'Walk for Whales' in North London. It is thanks to local groups giving time to campaigning and fund-raising that Greenpeace can spread its message about environmental danger.**

WORK WITH COMPANIES AND GOVERNMENTS

Greenpeace tries to convince people that we cannot go on destroying the world we live in. This means trying to persuade companies to make products without damaging the **environment**, or saying to the UK government that it has a duty to pass laws about **clean production** and to enforce them.

▲ **Greenpeace people offering an *ozone-friendly* fridge to the Belgian environment minister. This was a campaign which was won thanks to companies like Calor Gas introducing a fridge coolant which does not destroy the *ozone layer* or cause climate change.**

There are green solutions to most environmental problems.

In 1997 the UK will take part in the International Climate Convention to discuss what to do about climate change and the damage from burning **fossil fuels** worldwide.

SOLVING PROBLEMS

There are different ways of solving environmental problems. Greenpeace organizes protests on land and at sea and talks to businesses and politicians. Trying to persuade powerful people about issues is called **lobbying**. Some lobbying is easy, some is more difficult. In 1996, Greenpeace persuaded supermarkets and McVitie's to use vegetable oil instead of fish oil in biscuits and margarine. This was to protect marine life which was being threatened by over-fishing. Other work, like encouraging people to switch to **solar power**, will take longer.

▼ **Dressing up as packets of digestive biscuits attracts public attention. This visit by Greenpeace protesters at 6.00am at the factory gates persuaded McVitie's to stop using fish oil.**

Calor Gas was the first company to make eco-friendly fridge coolants in Britain.

WORK IN CAMPAIGNING

Children on a beach in New Zealand wearing protective clothing and using sunscreen. New Zealand is particularly affected by the ozone hole in Antarctica.

The **ozone layer** provides a protective band of gases around the globe which shields us from the sun's harmful ultra-violet rays. Since the 1930s gases produced in aerosol sprays, **polystyrene foam** and fridges have all contributed to making an enormous hole in the ozone layer. This means that you have to protect yourself more and more against the sun's rays.

'GREENFREEZE'

In 1990 Greenpeace started its **'greenfreeze'** campaign against ozone-destroying gases in fridges and freezers. It took five years for most fridge companies to change to methods which did not damage the ozone layer. Now these better methods have spread around the world from China to Argentina. However, scientists say: 'We cannot expect the ozone layer to return to normal until late into the next century'.

Most fridge companies now use a cheap, green coolant when they build fridges.

The Greenpeace truck outside Tesco's protesting against the damage to the ozone layer. The long-term solution to repairing the ozone hole is the production of 'greenfreeze' fridges and freezers which Tesco's have begun to try out.

Children in the UK presented a petition to the Prime Minister in 1992 with drawings of the ozone hole.

The ozone hole over Antarctica is the size of North America.

WORK IN COMMUNICATIONS

◀ The *Rainbow Warrior* and an international peace fleet sailed to the edge of the Mururoa *exclusion zone*. The world was told that two Greenpeace activists had managed to hide on the *atoll* itself to delay the test.

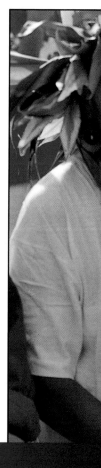

Modern **communications** are very important to Greenpeace campaigning. Offices across the world have to communicate with each other and with the world media. The 'squisher' is a computer used by Greenpeace to receive and send sound, photos and action film. It 'squishes' information into digital form, which appears on televisions miles away at exactly the same time. TV news sometimes shows Greenpeace **protest** actions almost as they happen.

INSTANT NEWS

In 1995, the 'squisher' helped to communicate the worldwide protest against French underground nuclear testing at the Mururoa atoll in the South Pacific. The protest was difficult and long. Greenpeace campaigners sailed into the testing zone to draw attention to the risks to people and to the coral reef. The protest spread all over the world. Ordinary people demonstrated against the nuclear tests.

The Mururoa atoll has started to sink as a result of 124 nuclear tests.

► French commandoes stormed the *Rainbow Warrior* inside the exclusion zone by using tear gas and overpowering the crew. As they did this, film and photos were sent to the world outside through the 'squisher'.

▼ Thousands of people living on the Cook Islands, in the Pacific, marched in protest against the French nuclear tests.

As the Greenpeace ships sailed into the French exclusion zone, the 'squisher' sent news from the *Rainbow Warrior*. The world knew straight away when the Greenpeace ships were seized by the French navy. Thousands of Tahitians heard the message and protested. They spread the news using their traditional way of communicating – conch shells.

The South Pacific campaign convinced ordinary people that it was up to them to make themselves heard. In 1996, the Comprehensive Test Ban Treaty was finally signed in New York.

Three out of four French people were against

THE BRENT SPAR
CAMPAIGN

Brent Spar is an oil rig weighing 14,500 tonnes. For many years it was a storage **depot** for oil in the North Sea, from which the oil was shipped onto land. By 1995 the oil rig was getting old and Shell decided to dump it in the Atlantic. This decision led to a protest in Europe.

DUMPING AT SEA

Dumping rubbish at sea goes against common sense. There are 400 other rigs in the North Sea. They all contain **heavy metals**, poisonous waste and oil. Nobody knows what would happen to marine wildlife if they were all dumped. Greenpeace warned against taking risks with the marine **environment**. They asked: 'What is the point of taking old tins to the can bank when Shell is going to dump its rubbish in the sea?'

To try to stop the dumping, Greenpeace decided to attract attention by occupying the rig. Living on the rig was hard. It was cold and dark. The protesters changed over every few days. They had to rely on fresh supplies being brought in by helicopter or in inflatable dinghies. Sometimes they had to suffer being sprayed by water hoses from Shell's ships. After 24 days the Greenpeace volunteers had to give in. However, the struggle on the rig had inspired ordinary people in the rest of Europe.

Greenpeace protesters climbed aboard the oil platform to tell the world that Shell intended to dump it 2000 metres down in the Atlantic. By the end of the campaign one of Shell's directors said: 'Greenpeace made deepwater disposal a symbol of man's misuse of the clean seas.'

The European Commission report said that most oil rigs could be recycled.

PROTEST IN EUROPE

In Germany and the Netherlands there were protests by politicians of all parties against the sinking of the Brent Spar. Many people were furious about a big international company dumping waste in the sea and **boycotted** Shell garages. Finally, Shell decided to tow the rig back into a quiet **fjord** and plan how to take it apart. The company is looking at six possible ways of reusing the rigs, none of which includes dumping at sea. Finally, 11 environment ministers at the North Sea Conference promised to stop the oil rigs being sunk. For the time being, all dumping has been stopped and there may be a permanent ban soon.

In 1996, Greenpeace organized a conference called 'Brent Spar and after' for people from leading companies to discuss solutions to **environmental problems**. Greenpeace director Peter Melchett said: 'The new environmental struggle is to put solutions into practice.'

▲ In the end, Greenpeace protesters were taken away, but one British newspaper, *The Financial Times*, wrote that ordinary people were now just as likely, if not more likely, to trust people from Greenpeace, as they were to trust people from the government or big businesses.

▼ On 20 June, 1995, Shell told the tugs to tow the Brent Spar to a Norwegian fjord. Swedish and German environment ministers were delighted and said: 'This shows that it is worth protesting.'

Recycling or reusing old rigs will create jobs.

VISION FOR THE FUTURE

The good news is that there are ways to prevent the destruction of the Earth. For instance, Greenpeace is working on practical ways of making the sun provide the electricity we need. Although new equipment to produce **solar power** costs money, solar energy is free, unlimited and does not cause **pollution**.

It is possible that a solar power plant will be built on the island of Crete to provide electricity. 'We have a real chance for the first time anywhere to replace a **fossil fuel** plant with a solar-powered scheme,' says Jeremy Leggett, a Greenpeace solar campaigner.

Even in ancient times, people knew about the immense power of the sun. It provides us with light, heat and the means for growing our food. Now at last we know how to capture its rays for electricity. The power station on Crete could become the inspiration for a new kind of non-polluting energy all round the world.

Japan will build 70,000 homes with solar panels by the year 2000.

This solar-powered house uses 48 panels on its south-facing roof. The sun's rays can produce unlimited amounts of electricity even in countries which are not particularly sunny.

Light bulbs which save electricity are being used more and more for homes and public places. The Bay Bridge between San Francisco and Oakland, one of the most beautiful bridges in the world, is now lit with energy-saving light bulbs.

The Twingo 'Smile' is a non-petrol-guzzling car. Greenpeace worked with an engineering company to produce this model, based on the Renault Twingo, which uses half the petrol of an ordinary car.

Cars using less petrol will cut pollution.

FURTHER INFORMATION

Greenpeace receives many requests for information about its activities. In response to enquiries Greenpeace provides leaflets on a variety of current issues and campaigns. Current material contains information about:

- toxic pollution of rivers and seas, including the problem with chemicals like PVC

- nuclear threats from weapons and nuclear power and reprocessing

- climate change due to the burning of fossil fuels in power stations and cars

- plants and animals threatened by destruction of habitats and exploitation

- solutions to environmental problems such as solar power, which can satisfy two-thirds of Britain's electricity needs

Greenwitness is a schools project which aims to involve students in obtaining oral information about the environment from older people. Greenpeace provides resources for teachers wishing to introduce the project to their students.

In addition, Greenpeace provides an information leaflet about its own activities including a listing of its international offices, as well as a signpost directory of other environmental organizations.

For further information please contact:

Greenpeace Information
Canonbury Villas
London N1 2PN
tel 0171 865 8100
fax 0171 865 8200
Web site:
http://www.greenpeace.org/UK

GLOSSARY

atoll a circular coral reef sticking out in the open sea and creating a separate lagoon or pool

boycott refuse to buy a product

clean production a way of making the things we need without using toxic materials. It aims to use as little energy as possible.

clearcutting one of the most harmful forest cutting methods. It removes all plant life and every tree from a given area.

communications ways of sending information to other places. They include post, telephone, computer and satellite.

depot storage place; in the case of oil rigs a place where crude oil is kept before it is piped to refineries

eco-friendly harmless to life forms in their natural environment

environment the surroundings in which living creatures live, like seas, rivers, forests, air, or buildings in towns and cities

environmental problems caused by damage done to the environment by pollution

exclusion zone an area of air or sea declared out of bounds for reasons of national security

fjord a sea inlet

fossil fuels gas, coal and oil. They are called 'non-renewable' because they have built up over millions of years and cannot be replaced.

genetic experiment altering the nature of a plant by adding or taking away certain genes

genetically manipulated having undergone a gene alteration

global warming the Earth's climates getting hotter as gases build up in the atmosphere

green not harmful to the natural environment

greenfreeze fridge coolant which uses hydrocarbon gases instead of CFCs, HCFCs and HFCs

heavy metals poisonous chemicals used in industrial processes and in everyday products such as batteries and paints. They include lead, mercury, cadmium and chromium which cannot be incinerated.

lobbying negotiating with politicians and other powerful people

nuclear energy produced through splitting minerals such as uranium. The energy produced once seemed a cheap and clean alternative to coal and oil. But now we know it is not safe.

nuclear weapons the most deadly weapons known, which can kill up to half a million people at one stroke

ozone-friendly gas or chemical which does not harm the ozone layer

ozone layer a protective layer around the earth's surface, which filters the sun's harmful rays

plankton tiny animals and plants which serve as food for fish. The toxic waste absorbed by plankton is then passed on through the food chain.

pollution poisoning or harming any part of the environment

polystyrene foam an insulating material used for packaging and disposable cups

protest a demonstration or other activity designed to draw attention to environmental danger

PVC (short for polyvinylchloride) a widely used plastic, which leaks toxic chemicals while it is being made or used, and which is dangerous when burnt

quota limiting fish catches to stop overfishing

solar power the energy that can be produced from the sun

temperate rainforest rainforests in North America, Canada and also Chile and New Zealand. There are fewer temperate than tropical rainforests and they have suffered even greater destruction.

toxic poisonous

wind power the energy that can be produced from the wind

INDEX